SPIRITUAL WARFARE

Volume 1

Copyright © 2024 Dr. Sylvia Blessings

All rights reserved. No part of this publication may be reproduced, distributed, or transmitted in any form or by any means, including photocopying, recording, or other electronic or mechanical methods, without prior written permission of the publisher.

Scriptures in this book are quoted from the following versions: King James Version (KJV) Public Domain

ISBN 979-8-9922558-1-2

Publisher Sylvia Blessings

Printed in the United States of America

For inquiries or permissions, contact sylvia.blessings@aol.com

DEDICATION

To all those who have courageously faced the battles of life, embracing the power of prayer and the unwavering strength of faith. May this book be a beacon of hope, a guide to victory, and a testament to the enduring love and faithfulness of our Heavenly Father.

CONTENTS

01
UNDERSTANDING SPIRITUAL WARFARE P.13

02
IDENTIFYING THE ENEMY P.19

03
OUR SPIRITUAL DEFENSE P.27

04
THE POWER OF PRAYER IN WARFARE P.33

05
TESTIMONIES OF TRIUMPH P.39

06
CONFRONTING WITCHCRAFT AND EVIL POWERS P.48

07
BREAKING DEMONIC STRONGHOLD P.55

08
THE ROLE OF FAITH IN DELIVERANCE P.66

09
OVERCOMING FEAR AND DOUBT P.71

10
STORIES OF LIGHT IN DARKNESS P.78

11
DELIVERANCE FROM SETBACK AND STAGNATION P.83

12
PRAYERS FOR OVERCOMING DELAYS P.93

13
HEALING FROM PAST WOUNDS P.98

PREFACE

The world we live in is often filled with unseen forces and spiritual battles that rage around us. Many find themselves entangled in struggles, facing delays, setbacks, and disappointments, questioning the presence of God in their lives. It's in these moments of uncertainty, fear, and pain that we need a lifeline, a source of hope and unwavering strength.

This book is a testament to the unwavering power of prayer and the unwavering presence of God in our lives. It's a guide for spiritual warriors, a tool to equip you with the knowledge and tools needed to overcome the challenges and obstacles that stand in your way. Through-out these pages, you will find a collection of potent prayers, specific prayer points, and relevant biblical verses designed to confront and conquer the enemy. These spiritual weapons are your arsenal against the forces of darkness, providing you with the tools to break free from chains, seek healing, and experience the favor and blessings of God.

My desire is that this book becomes a companion on your spiritual journey, a source of encouragement, and a reminder that you are never alone in this battle. May this book be a beacon of hope, a guide to victory, and a testament to the enduring love and

faithfulness of our Heavenly Father.

ACKNOWLEDGEMENTS

First and foremost, I want to express my heartfelt gratitude to God, the source of all wisdom and grace, for the inspiration and guidance that made this book possible. His unwavering love and strength have been my constant companions throughout this journey. I am deeply indebted to my family and friends for their unwavering support and encouragement. Their belief in my vision and their prayers have been a source of strength during moments of doubt and challenge. I also extend my thanks to the many individuals who have shared their testimonies and experiences of spiritual warfare, offering valuable insights and inspiring stories. Their courage and resilience have enriched this book and empowered countless others. Finally, I would like to acknowledge all the readers who have sought knowledge and empowerment through spiritual warfare. Your thirst for truth and commitment to seeking God's favor have been a constant source of inspiration. May this book be a source of strength and guidance on your spiritual journey.

INTRODUCTION

The spiritual realm is a reality we cannot ignore. In this realm, unseen forces, angelic beings, and demonic spirits constantly battle for our souls. We are not merely physical beings; we are also spiritual beings, intricately connected to the world beyond our physical senses. Within this book, we embark on a journey into the heart of spiritual warfare, recognizing the spiritual battles that we face as believers. We will explore the power of prayer as our most potent weapon, a weapon that can shatter chains, break down strongholds, and usher in healing, favor, and prosperity. These pages contain prayers that are not merely words to recite; they express our faith, declare our dependence on God, and proclaim His sovereignty over our lives.

This book is not a magic spell but a guide to understanding the realities of the spiritual realm and how we can navigate those realities through faith and prayer. It will equip you with the knowledge and tools you need to conquer the enemy, experience breakthroughs, and walk in victory. As we delve deeper into this realm, I invite you to open your heart to the power of prayer, to embrace the truth of God's presence, and to trust in His unwavering love and protection.

Chapter 01
Understanding Spiritual Warfare

Spiritual warfare, a phrase that may conjure images of dramatic battles and supernatural forces, is a very real and vital element of the Christian faith. It's not something that only a select few experience, but a reality that every believer encounters in their journey. It's the unseen conflict that rages around us, a struggle between the forces of light and darkness,

Chapter 01

good and evil, God and the enemy. Understanding this spiritual battle is not about becoming obsessed with the demonic or living in fear, but about gaining clarity and equipping ourselves with the tools necessary to overcome the challenges we face. The Bible is clear: we engage in a cosmic war, and as Christians, we must fight not with earthly weapons but with the power of God.

Paul, in his letter to the Ephesians, vividly describes this spiritual warfare: "For we are not fighting against flesh and blood, but against the rulers, against the authorities, against the powers of this dark world and against the spiritual forces of evil in the heavenly realms." This is not simply an abstract concept but a reality that manifests in the challenges, trials, and setbacks we encounter in our lives. Think

Chapter 01

about the daily battles we face – temptations, doubts, anxieties, fear, bitterness, and anger. These aren't just random emotions, but often expressions of spiritual attacks. We may experience unexpected delays in our goals, setbacks in our relationships, or even physical illnesses – these can all be manifestations of spiritual warfare. It's not always about grand pronouncements of evil, but the subtle, persistent whispers of doubt and despair.

The enemy's strategy is to discourage, weaken, and ultimately destroy us. He seeks to steal our joy, our peace, and our hope, hindering our walk with God and preventing us from fulfilling our divine purpose. But the good news is that we are not helpless victims. God equips us with the weapons we

Chapter 01

need to win this war. The Bible equips us with a formidable arsenal of spiritual weapons. We are called to wear the Armor of God, a metaphorical armor of faith, righteousness, peace, truth, salvation, and the Word of God. This armor is not physical but spiritual, offering protection from the enemy's attacks and empowering us to stand firm in the face of adversity. The most potent weapon in our arsenal, however, is prayer.

Prayer is not simply a passive act of petitioning God, but a powerful weapon of warfare. Through prayer, we engage in a dialogue with the Almighty, accessing His power, wisdom, and protection. Prayer is a form of spiritual warfare, a means of commanding the enemy to retreat and claiming victory in the name of Jesus. Throughout this journey, we'll explore specific

Chapter 01

examples of spiritual warfare, the different strategies of the enemy, and the practical steps we can take to combat his schemes. We'll delve into the power of prayer, examining the various ways it can be used to overcome challenges and claim victory.

We'll learn how to identify and dismantle spiritual strongholds that hinder our progress and explore the vital role of faith in deliverance and healing. The battle may be fierce, but we are not alone. God has promised to fight for us, to protect us, and to give us victory.Through his power, we can stand firm in the face of adversity, overcome every obstacle, and experience the incredible freedom and joy that come from living a life of victory in Christ.

As we embark on this journey of

Chapter 01

understanding spiritual warfare, let us remember that we are not called to fight alone. We have the power of God within us, the guidance of His Word, and the support of the Holy Spirit. Let us embrace the truth of His victory, claim His promises, and walk forward in confidence, knowing that we are more than conquerors through Christ who loves us.

Chapter 02
Identifying the Enemy

The reality of spiritual warfare is not a mere concept confined to ancient scriptures; it's a living, breathing experience that impacts our lives daily. It's not a distant battlefield fought by unseen forces. It's a struggle in our hearts, in our challenges, and in the whispers of doubt that seek to steal our joy. We constantly battle unseen forces, and we can't ignore this truth. Think of it like this: Imagine yourself walking through a vast forest. It's beautiful, serene, filled with vibrant life, but beneath

Chapter 02

the surface, hidden from plain sight, are unseen dangers. Lurking in the shadows are wild animals, venomous snakes, and unseen traps. Just as you navigate this hidden world with caution, so too must we navigate the spiritual realm. But unlike the physical forest, the spiritual realm is a battleground where our very souls are at stake.

Our enemy, the devil, is a cunning strategist, a master deceiver, whose sole purpose is to steal, kill, and destroy. He doesn't fight fair; he relies on deceit, fear, and lies to break our spirit and steer us off course. So, how do we identify this enemy? How do we discern the subtle whispers of his deceit from the gentle guidance of the Holy Spirit? First, we must recognize the enemy's tactics. He uses a range of methods to infiltrate our lives, each designed to weaken our faith and draw us away from God's will.

The Arsenal of Darkness: Deception: The enemy often disguises his attacks, making them appear as simple misfortunes, setbacks, or even blessings. He might masquerade

Chapter 02

as a trusted friend, a well-meaning advisor, or even a seemingly innocent opportunity. He whispers doubts, planting seeds of fear, and presenting alternative paths that seem alluring but ultimately lead to destruction.

Fear: Fear is a potent weapon that paralyzes our faith and steals our joy. The enemy loves to instill fear, whether it be fear of the unknown, fear of failure, fear of rejection, or fear of losing loved ones. He knows that fear is the antithesis of faith, and he'll use it to keep us trapped in a cycle of anxiety and worry.

Accusation: The enemy constantly seeks to condemn us, reminding us of our past mistakes and failures. He whispers doubts about our worth, our ability to overcome, and our very salvation. He loves to paint a picture of hopelessness, ensuring we believe we are beyond redemption.

Distraction: The enemy loves to keep us busy, diverting our attention from what truly matters. He tempts us with worldly pleasures, distractions, and fleeting pursuits that consume our time and energy, leaving little room for spiritual growth and

Chapter 02

reflection.

Discouragement: The enemy's ultimate goal is to discourage us, to make us believe that our efforts are futile and that God has abandoned us. He whispers lies about our inadequacies, our lack of progress, and our inability to achieve victory.

Signs of a Spiritual Attack: Recognizing the enemy's tactics is crucial, but so is recognizing the signs of his attacks. These signs can be subtle, manifesting as a shift in our emotions, thoughts, or behaviors.

Uncharacteristic Anxiety and Fear: A persistent feeling of unease, dread, or fear that seems unwarranted, even crippling. This could be accompanied by insomnia, racing thoughts, or difficulty focusing.

Sudden Loss of Joy and Peace: A noticeable shift from inner peace to feelings of sadness, emptiness, or restlessness without a clear reason.

Increased Irritability and Anger: A sudden surge in temper, impatience, and negativity, leading to increased conflict and

Chapter 02

outbursts of anger.

Physical Discomfort or Ailments: The enemy can attack our physical well-being as a form of spiritual warfare, leading to unexplained aches, pains, and illnesses.

Recurring Negative Thoughts and Intrusive Images: Persistent thoughts of doubt, fear, and despair that seem impossible to shake off, even if you know they are illogical.

Inability to Pray or Connect with God: A sudden resistance to prayer or a feeling of disconnection from God, leading to a sense of spiritual coldness or apathy.

Increased Cravings for Sinful Behavior: A stronger urge to indulge in harmful habits, like addictions, gossip, or lustful thoughts. They're hard to resist.

Unwarranted Delays and Setbacks: A series of unforeseen obstacles and delays in areas of life that seem beyond your control, hindering your progress.

A Feeling of Hopelessness and Defeat: A deep sense of despair and discouragement, believing you're incapable of achieving

Chapter 02

your goals or overcoming challenges.

Dreams of Evil or Violence: Recurring dreams with disturbing or terrifying content, leaving you feeling uneasy or shaken.

It's important to note that not all difficulties in life are automatically spiritual attacks.

Some challenges are simply a part of the human experience, caused by natural circumstances or our own choices. However, when faced with persistent and seemingly inexplicable struggles, particularly those accompanied by the signs mentioned above, it's crucial to discern the source and seek spiritual protection.

Recognizing the Enemy's Authority: It's crucial to understand that the enemy has limited authority in our lives. He operates through deception, fear, and manipulation, but he can only attack us with the permission we unknowingly grant him.

We often give him authority by: Ignoring or denying God's Word: When we fail to actively seek and abide by God's instructions, we create a void in our lives that He can easily fill with His lies.

Chapter 02

Holding on to Unforgiveness: Unforgiveness allows the enemy to gain a foothold in our hearts, poisoning our relationships and hindering our spiritual growth.

Giving in to Fear and Doubt: When we succumb to fear and doubt, we cripple our faith and give the enemy the power to paralyze us.

Compromising Our Values: When we prioritize the desires of the flesh over God's will, we open ourselves to temptation and vulnerability.

Inability to Pray: When we can't pray, it can be interpreted as a spiritual struggle, a mental block, a symptom of mental illness, a rejection of your faith or religious belief in Christ, or simply a personal choice.

Claiming Back Your Authority: The good news is that we are not helpless in this spiritual battle. God has given us the power to overcome the enemy through faith, prayer, and the power of His Holy Spirit. By understanding the enemy's tactics and recognizing his attempts to infiltrate our lives, we can actively

Chapter 02

resist his influence and reclaim the authority that Christ has given us. Remember, the enemy is defeated. Christ's victory on the cross has already won the battle. We must simply walk in that victory, claiming the authority that is ours in Christ. The battle against the forces of darkness is not a solo mission. We need the support of our brothers and sisters in Christ, the guidance of wise mentors, and the unwavering strength that comes from drawing closer to God. We must be vigilant, discerning, and unwavering in our faith, for we are not fighting alone. God is with us, and His power is greater than any darkness.

Chapter 03
Our Spiritual Defense

In the realm of spiritual warfare, we find ourselves engaged in a battle that transcends the physical realm. It is a battle against unseen forces, against principalities, against powers, against the rulers of the darkness of this age, against spiritual wickedness in high places (Ephesians 6:12). These enemies seek to hinder our growth, steal our joy, and ultimately lead us away from the path of righteousness. But God, in His infinite grace and mercy, has equipped us with

Chapter 03

the necessary tools to stand strong against these adversaries. One of the most crucial weapons in our spiritual arsenal is the Armor of God, described in Ephesians 6:10-18. Just as a soldier in earthly warfare relies on armor to protect himself, we, as soldiers of Christ, must be fully clad in God's divine protection. Each piece of armor represents a specific spiritual virtue that empowers us to overcome the enemy's attacks.

The Belt of Truth: The first piece of armor is the belt of truth, symbolizing the unwavering commitment to God's Word. It is our foundation, the bedrock upon which our faith stands firm. When we are grounded in truth, we resist the deceptive tactics of the enemy. His lies lose their power when we are rooted in God's infallible Word. We must diligently study the Scriptures, allowing them to permeate our hearts and minds so that we are able to discern truth from falsehood.

The Breastplate of Righteousness: The breastplate of righteousness is the second piece of armor, safeguarding our hearts and minds from the enemy's assaults. It represents our

Chapter 03

inner purity, our commitment to living a life that aligns with God's will. Righteousness is not merely about outward actions, but about the transformation of our hearts. It is the inner conviction that guides our choices and motives. When we are clothed in righteousness, we are protected from the enemy's accusations and condemnation.

The Shoes of the Gospel of Peace: The shoes of the gospel of peace enable us to move with confidence and purpose in the face of adversity. They symbolize the peace that surpasses all understanding, the peace that comes from knowing Jesus as our Lord and Savior. Peace is not simply the absence of conflict, but a deep inner tranquility that enables us to stand firm amidst storms. When we walk in the shoes of peace, we spread the message of reconciliation and hope, dispelling the darkness with the light of the gospel.

The Shield of Faith: The shield of faith is our ultimate defense against the fiery darts of the enemy. It represents our unwavering belief in the power and promises of God. In

Chapter 03

defense against the fiery darts of the enemy. It represents our unwavering belief in the power and promises of God. In the face of doubt and fear, faith is our shield, quenching the fiery arrows of accusation, despair, and hopelessness. It is through faith that we receive God's protection, His strength, and His unwavering love.

The Helmet of Salvation: The helmet of salvation protects our minds from the enemy's attacks on our thoughts and beliefs. Salvation is not merely a one-time event, but an ongoing process of surrender and transformation. It is the assurance that we are eternally secure in God's love and grace. When we wear the helmet of salvation, we are protected from the enemy's attempts to instill fear, doubt, and despair.

The Sword of the Spirit: The sword of the Spirit is the weapon that we wield in spiritual warfare. It is the Word of God, the ultimate weapon against the forces of darkness. The Bible contains the truths, promises, and power of God,

Chapter 03

which enable us to overcome every obstacle. By studying the Word, meditating on it, and applying it to our lives, we are empowered to resist the enemy's attacks and advance the Kingdom of God.

The Power of Prayer: While the Armor of God equips us for battle, prayer is the fuel that keeps our spiritual engine running. Prayer is our communication with God, our lifeline to His strength, and our source of hope. Through prayer, we can access the power of the Holy Spirit, allowing Him to empower us to stand firm in the face of adversity. Prayer is not merely a request list, but a conversation with our Heavenly Father, an opportunity to draw near to Him and experience His presence in our lives.

The Importance of Community: In the context of spiritual warfare, we are not meant to fight alone. We need the support of our brothers and sisters in Christ. A strong spiritual community provides encouragement, accountability,and a united front against the enemy. We must be willing to share

Chapter 03

our struggles, pray for one another, and stand together in faith.

Testimonies of Triumph: Throughout history, countless individuals have triumphed over spiritual challenges through faith and prayer. Their stories are a testament to the power of God, and they serve as a source of inspiration and encouragement. We learn from their experiences, draw strength from their victories, and remember that we too can overcome any obstacle with God's help.

The battle against spiritual wickedness is real, but we are not alone. God has given us the Armor of God, a complete suit of protection, and the power of prayer to stand firm against the enemy. By putting on this armor, by drawing strength from God's Word, and by relying on the power of prayer, we can be victorious in every spiritual battle.

Chapter 04
The Power of Prayer in Warfare

In the realm of spiritual warfare, where unseen forces clash, prayer emerges as a formidable weapon, a potent force capable of dismantling strongholds, breaking chains, and ushering in divine intervention. It is a lifeline that connects us to the very heart of God, our ultimate source of strength, guidance, and victory. Just as a soldier relies on their arsenal to overcome the enemy, so too must we equip ourselves with the power of prayer to navigate the battles of our souls. Imagine yourself

Chapter 04

standing on the front lines of a spiritual confrontation. The enemy, shrouded in darkness, seeks to exploit our weaknesses, sow seeds of doubt, and hinder our progress. But we are not defenseless. We possess a weapon far more potent than any earthly weapon – the weapon of prayer. It is a communication line, a bridge that connects us to the divine power that can shatter the enemy's plans. Scripture itself reveals the potent nature of prayer in spiritual warfare. The apostle Paul exhorts us to "pray without ceasing" (1 Thessalonians 5:17). This constant communion with God strengthens our faith and equips us to stand firm against the assaults of the enemy. Just as a continuous supply of ammunition strengthens an army, so too does consistent prayer fortify our spiritual defenses.

Prayer is not merely a passive act of supplication. It is an active engagement with God, a dynamic exchange of power. We speak to God, pouring out our hearts, revealing our needs, and seeking His guidance. We intercede on behalf of others, lifting them up in prayer and wielding the power of others, lifting them up in

Chapter 04

prayer and wielding the power of intercession to bring healing and deliverance. And in doing so, we tap into the very essence of God's power, unleashing His mighty hand to work on our behalf.

Consider the words of Jesus himself: "Truly I tell you, if you have faith as small as a mustard seed, you can say to this mountain, 'Move from here to there,' and it will move. Nothing will be impossible for you" (Matthew 17:20). This powerful verse underscores the inherent power that lies within our faith and the role of prayer in amplifying it.

Through prayer, we call upon the very essence of God's power, drawing on the unlimited potential of His grace and mercy. Yet, people do not simply recite prayer as a formula. It is a heartfelt communion, a conversation with the Almighty. It is a pouring out of our souls, a relinquishment of our burdens, and a desperate cry for His guidance and intervention. In the depths of our despair, prayer becomes our anchor, a beacon of hope amidst the storm. It is the very breath of our spirits, the fuel

Chapter 04

that propels us forward in the face of adversity.

The efficacy of prayer is not dependent on our eloquence or our ability to craft perfect petitions. It is the sincerity of our hearts, the unwavering faith that fuels our prayers, that unlocks the divine power. When we pray with genuine conviction, with a heart full of longing for God's will, our prayers ascend to the heavens, piercing through the veils of darkness and reaching the ears of the Almighty. Imagine a battleground filled with darkness and despair. The enemy, armed with fear, doubt, and despair, attempts to crush the spirit of the believer. But amidst the chaos, a flicker of light emerges, a beacon of hope – a prayer. As the believer raises their hands in supplication, a symphony of intercession fills the air. Angelic armies descend, wielding the power of God's love to overcome the enemy's forces.

Prayer is a weapon of faith, a shield of protection, and a lifeline of hope. It is the voice of the believer, reaching out to

Chapter 04

a lifeline of hope. It is the voice of the believer, reaching out to the Almighty, seeking His grace, His guidance, and His power. It is the very essence of spiritual warfare, a testament to the unwavering strength of faith and the indomitable spirit of the believer.

    Throughout the pages of this book, we will delve into the power of prayer in overcoming various challenges, from battling demonic influences to achieving breakthroughs in every area of life. We will explore the importance of prayer in dismantling strongholds, breaking chains, and securing divine protection. We will equip ourselves with the spiritual weapons of prayer, wielding them with confidence and unwavering faith. But prayer is not a solitary endeavor. It is a tapestry woven together by the voices of countless believers, united in a common purpose. When we join hands in prayer, our voices rise in a chorus of intercession, creating a symphony of power that echoes through the heavens. Together, we form a formidable army that stands against the forces of darkness. We wield the weapon of prayer to

Chapter 04

bring about healing, deliverance, and victory, creating a force that others must reckon with. Let us embrace the power of prayer, not as a mere formality, but as a lifeline, a weapon, a testament to our faith, and a source of unwavering hope in the face of adversity. In the battlegrounds of our souls, prayer is our ultimate shield, our greatest weapon, and our constant companion on the path to victory.

Chapter 05
Testimonies of Triumph

In the tapestry of our spiritual journeys, we encounter moments of triumph that ignite our faith and inspire those around us. These victories, often born from battles fought in the unseen realm, are testaments to the power of prayer, the unwavering love of God, and the unwavering strength of the human spirit. Let us delve into the stories of those who have faced spiritual challenges head-on, emerging stronger, empowered, and filled with unshakeable hope.

Chapter 05

Mary's Healing and Unwavering Faith

I remember Mary from Maryland, a young woman brimming with dreams and aspirations, who found her life thrown into turmoil when a debilitating illness gripped her. Doctors offered little hope, and the weight of despair threatened to consume her. But Mary, rooted in her faith, refused to succumb to the darkness and the workers of evil. She sought refuge in prayer at (SBM), pouring out her heart to God, asking for healing and a miracle. She filled her days with fervent supplications and spent her nights in quiet trust in the Lord's unwavering love. She clung to the promises found in the Scriptures, drawing strength from verses like Psalm 103:3, "He heals all your diseases."

Though the battle was long and arduous, Mary never wavered in her faith. She immersed herself in prayer, seeking comfort in fellowship with SYLVIA BLESSINGS MINISTRIES (SBM) and drawing strength from me and the stories of others who had experienced miraculous healings at

Chapter 05

SYLVIA BLESSINGS MINISTRIES (SBM).

One day, in 2022 during our 100 days of prayer, she connected her faith to one of our warfare prayers online, praying with unwavering conviction; a sense of peace washed over her. A profound sense of calm replaced the anxiety that had plagued her. She felt a deep conviction that God had heard her prayers and was working in her life.

As days turned into weeks, the debilitating illness began to recede. Her strength returned, her spirit soared, and a radiant light shone in her eyes. Mary's story is a powerful testament to the efficacy of prayer, demonstrating that even in the darkest hours, God's grace is available, and His healing power can work wonders in our lives.

John's Deliverance from Addiction

John, a man once ensnared by the chains of addiction, found himself consumed by a darkness (spiritual wickedness) that threatened to consume his soul. He felt powerless against the pull of his desires, yearning for

Chapter 05

freedom but unable to break free on his own. Driven to despair, John turned to God by joining (SBM) and coming to me for God's guidance, seeking the strength he desperately needed. He and I began to pray, not with a sense of entitlement but with hearts overflowing with humility and desperation. He confessed his sins, acknowledged his weakness, and begged for God's mercy. He always joined my teachings and prayers on Facebook, finding solace and encouragement in the prayers and teachings he understood during his struggles. He immersed himself in prayer and the Word of God, finding solace and direction in the Scriptures. He leaned on the promise of 1 Corinthians 10:13, "No temptation has overtaken you that is not common to man. God is faithful, and He will not allow you to face temptation beyond your ability. With the temptation, He will also provide the way of escape so that you can endure it." As John continued to pray and seek God's guidance, he felt a shift within him. His cravings began to lessen, his willpower

Chapter 05

strengthened, and the darkness that had enveloped him slowly receded. He discovered a newfound strength, a determination to live a life free from addiction. His testimony serves as a beacon of hope, showing us that even the most seemingly insurmountable battles can be overcome through prayer, faith, perseverance, and God's unwavering love.

Susana's Journey to Forgiveness

Susana, one of my daughters in the faith, burdened by the weight of unforgiveness, felt trapped in a prison of bitterness and resentment. She had been hurt deeply by the actions of her husband, and the pain had festered within her, poisoning her thoughts, her emotions, and her relationships. She knew that holding onto unforgiveness was harming her more than anyone else, but she struggled to let go of the anger that consumed her. She turned to prayer because I told her it was an attack from the enemy to take away her joy and peace. In seeking God's guidance and strength to forgive the husband who had wronged her. She studied scriptures like Matthew 6:14-15, "For if you

Chapter 05

forgive men their trespasses, your heavenly Father will also forgive you. But if you do not forgive men their trespasses, neither will your Father forgive your trespasses."

The path to forgiveness was arduous, but Susana persevered. She learned to confront the painful memories, acknowledging the hurt she had endured while also seeking to understand the perspective of the one who had hurt her. She prayed for healing, not only for herself but for the one who had wronged her. Slowly, with each prayer, with each act of compassion towards herself and others, Susana felt the grip of bitterness loosen. The weight of unforgiveness began to lift, and she discovered a wellspring of forgiveness within her. Her journey, filled with tears and moments of doubt, ultimately led to a profound peace and the freedom that comes with letting go of the past. Susana's story underscores the liberating power of forgiveness. It reminds us that forgiveness is not a sign of weakness but a testament to our strength and our capacity for love.

Chapter 05

Emily's Breakthrough in Prayer

Emily, a woman facing a formidable challenge in her career, felt overwhelmed by the weight of her responsibilities and the pressures she faced. Evil powers and workers of iniquity have hijacked her career. She resorted to prayer and sought guidance and support from (SBM), turning to prayer as a source of strength and hope. Engaging in spiritual warfare through the altar of God at Sylvia Blessings Ministries (SBM). Her prayers were fervent and potent in the realm of the spirit; she fought a good fight of faith and never stopped there. She longed for a deeper connection with God, a sense of assurance that her prayers were being heard and answered. One evening, in one of our prayer conferences held every year, a profound sense of peace settled over her. She felt the presence of God all over her as I was leading prayer, an overwhelming sense of God's love, power, strength, and favor. Suddenly, she felt her heart overflow with gratitude, knowing and having a deep sense of conviction

Chapter 05

that she had won the battle over her career. After the conference, she had a breakthrough job. Emily's breakthrough in warfare prayer was a turning point in her life. She discovered a deeper intimacy with God, a connection that filled her with strength, courage, and a sense of unshakeable peace. Her story highlights the importance of prayer, not as a mere ritual but as a means of deepening our relationship with God, seeking His guidance, and receiving His strength.

The Power of Collective Prayer

Beyond individual testimonies, the power of collective prayer is undeniable. When believers gather together, united in their faith and purpose, their prayers take on profound significance. The book of Acts provides countless examples of the transformative power of united prayer. In Acts 4:24, we read, "When they heard this, they raised their voices together in prayer to God. 'Sovereign Lord,' they said, 'You made the heavens and the earth and the sea and everything in them."

Chapter 05

These verses describe a community of believers coming together to pray for strength, guidance, and protection. Their unified prayers led to an outpouring of the Holy Spirit, empowering them to overcome obstacles and spread the gospel with boldness.

The Promise of Victory

The testimonies of those who have overcome spiritual challenges offer a powerful reminder that we are not alone in our struggles. God is with us, fighting our battles and offering us the strength we need to overcome. Through prayer, through the fellowship of the church, and through the unwavering love of God, we can find the courage to confront the darkness and emerge victorious. Let the stories of those who have gone before us inspire us, empower us, and remind us of the profound power of prayer. For it is through faith, through the unwavering love of God, and through the strength found in prayer that we can conquer any challenge and experience the joy of spiritual victory.

Chapter 06
Confronting Witchcraft and Evil Powers

The world of witchcraft and demonic forces can be a terrifying and confusing place. It's easy to feel helpless and overwhelmed when faced with the darkness. But remember, you are not alone. You are a child of God, and He has given you everything you need to overcome these challenges. The Bible tells us that our struggle is not against flesh and blood, but against principalities, against powers, against the rulers of the darkness of this age, against spiritual hosts of

Chapter 06

wickedness in the heavenly places (Ephesians 6:12). These are real and powerful forces, but they are not invincible.

Our greatest weapon against these forces is the power of prayer. Prayer is a powerful tool that allows us to connect with God and draw upon His strength and protection. When we pray, we are not simply asking for something; we are aligning ourselves with God's will and tapping into His unlimited power.

Here are some practical strategies and prayers to combat witchcraft and evil forces:

Strategies:

Identify the Source: The first step in confronting witchcraft is identifying the source of the attack. This could be a person who practices witchcraft, a generational curse, or even a spiritual entity. You might need to seek guidance from a spiritual mentor or counselor.

Repent and Turn Away from Sin: The Bible says that sin gives the enemy a foothold in our lives. It's crucial to

Chapter 06

examine your own life for areas where you may be sinning and seek God's forgiveness and cleansing.

Declare Your Faith: The Word of God is a powerful weapon. Speak the Word over your life, declaring your faith in Jesus Christ and His power over all evil.

Break Curses: Curses are chains that can bind us to the influence of evil. It's essential to pray for the breaking of any curses that might be affecting you.

Cut Off Access to Your Life: You may need to sever any spiritual connections you have with the source of the witchcraft. This could involve cutting off relationships with people who practice witchcraft or getting rid of objects associated with the dark arts.

Cleanse Your Home: The presence of evil can manifest in a physical space. Cleanse your home through prayer and eliminate any items that may have associations with spiritual influences.

Powerful Prayers

Chapter 06

Prayer Against Witchcraft and Sorcery:

"Father, I come before You in the name of Jesus. I declare that I am a child of God, and I am covered by the blood of Jesus. I break the power of every curse, spell, and enchantment directed against me. I bind the power of every witch and sorcerer who has been working against me. I command them to leave my life, my family, and my home. Father, I ask You to protect me from every attack and keep me safe from the influence of evil. Amen."

Prayer for Protection:

"Lord, I ask you to surround me with your protective shield. Keep me safe from harm and deliver me from any evil spirits. I trust in your strength and your power to keep me safe. Amen."

Prayer to Break Demonic Strongholds:

"Jesus, I come to you in the name of the Father, the Son, and the Holy Spirit. I ask you to expose any demonic strongholds that are holding me captive. I break the power of these strongholds and command them to destroy themselves. I ask you to set me free from their influence. I will walk in freedom and victory. Amen."

Chapter 06

Prayer for Healing:

"Lord Jesus, I ask you to heal me from every sickness and disease. I declare that your healing power is available to me. I receive your healing power, and I am made whole in every area of my life. Amen."

Prayer for Deliverance:

"Lord, I come before You seeking Your deliverance. I renounce any demonic influence in my life. I break every chain and every yoke. I receive Your freedom, and I walk in the victory that You have won for me. Amen."

The Power of Faith:

Remember, the power of faith is crucial in this battle. When you pray, believe that God is hearing you and that He will answer your prayers. Don't let fear or doubt consume you. Focus on God's power and His love for you.

Testimonies of Victory:

Many people have experienced the power of prayer in overcoming witchcraft and demonic influence. Here are

Chapter 06

some testimonies:

Ama's Story: Ama had been battling fatigue, depression, and strange occurrences in her home. She felt drawn to the Bible and began to pray for deliverance. After weeks of dedicated prayer, she felt a sense of peace and liberation, and the strange occurrences stopped. Her energy and joy returned, and she was able to live a more peaceful and productive life.

Prince's Testimony: John had experienced a string of setbacks in his business. He felt like he was constantly fighting against unseen forces. He sought the advice of a spiritual mentor who encouraged him to pray for deliverance from demonic interference. John began to pray regularly and to study the Bible. He also began to implement strategies to protect himself and his business from further attacks. Within a few months, John experienced a turnaround in his business, and he attributed it to God's intervention.

Living in Victory:

The battle against witchcraft and evil forces is ongoing, but

Chapter 06

remember that you are not alone. God is with you, and He is fighting for you. By relying on His strength, seeking His guidance, and using the weapons of prayer and faith, you can experience victory over the darkness and live a life of freedom and abundance. The journey to spiritual victory may not always be easy, but it is possible. Trust in God's power and never give up. Remember, you are a child of God, and He has promised to be with you always.

Chapter 07
Breaking Demonic Stronghold

Demons are cunning adversaries, masters of deception and illusion. They seek to establish strongholds in our lives: places where they can control our thoughts, emotions, and actions. These strongholds are like fortresses, built on lies, fear, and past hurts. They can manifest in various forms, such as addiction, fear, bitterness, unforgiveness, and even physical ailments.

Imagine a fortress with high walls and impenetrable

Chapter 07

gates. This is what a demonic stronghold can feel like. It traps us within its confines, preventing us from experiencing the fullness of God's love and freedom. The enemy knows that if he can keep us captive, he can keep us from fulfilling our God-given purpose. However, just as a fortress can be breached, so too can demonic strongholds be dismantled. God has given us the authority and power to resist the devil and his schemes. He has provided us with weapons of spiritual warfare; most importantly, the power of prayer.

Steps to Identify and Dismantle Strongholds:

1. Self-Reflection and Examination:

- Begin by honestly examining your life. Identify areas where you feel stuck, trapped, or unable to move forward.
- Ask yourself questions like: What are my biggest struggles?
- What fears or anxieties hold me back?
- Where do I experience constant defeat or disappointment? Are there patterns of negative thoughts or behaviors in my life?

Chapter 07

- Have I experienced trauma or abuse that I haven't fully dealt with?
- Be honest and open with yourself. Don't try to hide or minimize your struggles.

2. Seek Guidance from God's Word: The Bible is a powerful tool in spiritual warfare. Spend time reading and meditating on verses related to spiritual freedom, deliverance, and overcoming strongholds.

Consider passages like:

Ephesians 6:10-18: "Finally, be strong in the Lord and in his mighty power. Put on the full armor of God, so that you can take your stand against the devil's schemes."

2 Corinthians 10:4-5: "The weapons we fight with are not the weapons of the world. On the contrary, they have divine power to demolish strongholds. We demolish arguments and every pretension that sets itself up against the knowledge of God, and we take captive every thought to make it obedient to Christ."

Chapter 07

- **Romans 8:37-39:** "No, in all these things we are more than conquerors through him who loved us. For I am convinced that neither death nor life, neither angels nor demons, neither the present nor the future, nor any powers, neither height nor depth, nor anything else in all creation, will be able to separate us from the love of God that is in Christ Jesus our Lord."
- Let the Word of God speak to your heart, reveal hidden truths, and equip you for battle.

3. Engage in Prayer and Fasting: Prayer is a powerful weapon against the forces of darkness. Dedicate time to fervent prayer, ask God to reveal the root of your strongholds and give you the strength to break them.

- Fasting can be a powerful tool for spiritual growth and deliverance. By abstaining from food or certain pleasures, we demonstrate our commitment to God and create space for spiritual insight and breakthrough.
- Prayer and fasting are a potent combination for spiritual warfare, opening our hearts and minds to the power of God.

Chapter 07

4. Repentance and Forgiveness: Demonic strongholds often have their roots in unconfessed sin, bitterness, unforgiveness, or past traumas.

- Seek God's forgiveness for your own sins and transgressions. Repent of any sin that may be fueling the stronghold.
- Practice forgiveness toward others, including yourself. Unforgiveness creates a space for the enemy to exploit bitterness and resentment.
- Forgiveness is a powerful act of spiritual release that can dismantle strongholds and pave the way for healing and freedom.

5. Renew Your Mind: - The enemy often attacks our minds with negative thoughts, lies, and self-defeating beliefs.

- Renew your mind with the truth of God's Word. Fill your mind with Scripture, uplifting music, and positive affirmations.
- Challenge negative thoughts and replace them with God's promises.
- Choose to focus on gratitude, hope, and faith.

Chapter 07

- By renewing your mind, you reclaim control over your thoughts and emotions, making it harder for the enemy to gain a foothold.

6. Seek Counsel and Support:

- Don't be afraid to seek guidance and support from a trusted spiritual leader or counselor.
- They can offer prayers, encouragement, and practical advice on how to break free from strongholds.
- Surround yourself with a community of believers who will pray for you and walk alongside you in your journey.

7. Embrace the Power of the Holy Spirit:

- The Holy Spirit is our greatest ally in spiritual warfare. He empowers us with strength, wisdom, and discernment.
- Invite the Holy Spirit to fill you with his power and
- presence. Yield to his guidance and let him direct your steps.
- He will equip you to resist temptation, combat evil, and experience the freedom that comes from breaking demonic strongholds.

Chapter 07

Breaking Strongholds through Specific Prayer Points:

Prayer for Revelation and Truth: "Lord, I ask for Your Holy Spirit to reveal the truth about the strongholds in my life. I want to understand how they came to be and how they are affecting me. I ask for Your wisdom and discernment to see the enemy's tactics clearly. Amen."

Prayer for Forgiveness and Healing: "Lord, I confess any sin that has opened the door to strongholds in my life. Forgive me for my transgressions and heal the wounds that have created vulnerabilities. I choose to forgive myself and others for past hurts and release them from my heart. Amen."

Prayer for Breaking the Power of the Stronghold: "Lord, I come against the strongholds in my life in the name of Jesus. I bind the powers of darkness that have held me captive. I break the chains of addiction, fear, bitterness, and unforgiveness. I release myself from their grip and claim my freedom in Christ. Amen."

Prayer for Filling with the Holy Spirit:

- "Lord, I ask for your Holy Spirit to fill me with your power

Chapter 07

and presence. I need your strength to overcome the enemy's schemes. I need your wisdom to discern his tactics. I need your love to heal my brokenness. Come and dwell in me, Holy Spirit. Amen."

Examples of Demonic Strongholds and How to Break Them:

1. Addiction

- **Root:** Often rooted in a desire to escape pain, loneliness, or boredom.
- **Breaking the Stronghold**: Seek professional help and support groups.
- Pray for God's grace and strength to resist temptation. Replace unhealthy habits with healthy alternatives.
- Find purpose and meaning in life outside of the addiction.

Prayer: "Lord, I come against the stronghold of addiction in my life. I repent of my choices and ask for Your forgiveness. Give me the strength to resist temptation and break free from this destructive cycle. I choose to live in freedom and purpose. Amen."

Chapter 07

2. Fear

- **Root:** Often stems from past experiences, insecurity, and a lack of trust in God.
- **Breaking the Stronghold:** Meditate on Scripture verses about God's love and protection.
- Engage in activities that build self-confidence and courage.
- Replace fearful thoughts with faith-filled ones.
- Ask God for the courage to face your fears.
- Prayer: "Lord, I am afraid. Please help me overcome my fears. I trust in your love and protection. I choose to believe that you are with me and that nothing can separate me from your love. Amen."

3. Bitterness

Root: Often arises from hurt, betrayal, or injustice.

Breaking the Stronghold: Practice forgiveness toward those who have wronged you.

- Choose to release the bitterness and allow God to heal the wounds.

Chapter 07

- Focus on gratitude and the positive aspects of your life.
- Seek counseling or support groups to process your pain.

Prayer: "Lord, I am bitter and resentful. I forgive those who have wronged me, and I release the bitterness from my heart. I choose to trust in your justice and grace. Heal my wounds and help me to love again. Amen."

4. Unforgiveness

- Root: Often rooted in pride, a desire for revenge, or a fear of letting go.
- Breaking the Stronghold: Understand that forgiveness is not about the other person, but about your own freedom.
- Pray for God to help you let go of the anger and resentment.
- Make a conscious decision to forgive, even if the other person doesn't deserve it.
- Seek guidance from a spiritual mentor or counselor.

Prayer: "Lord, I am holding onto unforgiveness. I know that this is harming me and preventing me from experiencing Your peace. Give me the strength to forgive those who have wronged me.

Chapter 07

Release me from the bitterness and resentment. I choose to trust in your justice and mercy. Amen."

Remember, breaking demonic strongholds is not a one- time event. It is an ongoing process that requires persistence, faith, and dependence on God. He is our ultimate victor, and with His help, we can overcome any challenge.

Chapter 08
The Role of Faith in Deliverance

Faith, the unwavering belief in the unseen, is the bedrock of our spiritual liberation. It is the invisible force that empowers us to overcome challenges, break free from demonic influences, and experience the transformative power of God in our lives. Just as a seed buried in the earth requires faith to believe that it will sprout and grow into a magnificent tree, our lives require faith to blossom into the fullness of God's purpose.

Imagine a small boat sailing across a vast ocean, encountering raging storms and towering waves. The

Chapter 08

tempestuous sea would surely swallow the boat if the anchor did not hold it firm. Similarly, our lives are like boats navigating the turbulent seas of life, and faith serves as our anchor, securing us against the storms of adversity. It is our lifeline to the divine, anchoring us to the unshakeable love and power of God.

The Bible is replete with stories of individuals who conquered overwhelming odds and achieved remarkable feats through unwavering faith. At the advanced age of 100, God commanded Abraham to leave his homeland and journey to a foreign land. With unwavering faith, he obeyed, demonstrating his trust in God's promises. His act of faith led to the birth of Isaac, the foundation of a nation blessed by God.

David, a young shepherd boy, faced the giant Goliath, armed only with his slingshot and unwavering faith in God. Despite the towering Goliath's imposing stature and formidable weaponry, David's faith in God's power propelled him to victory. The story of David and Goliath serves as a powerful reminder that our faith is not measured by our physical strength but by our trust in God's limitless power.

Chapter 08

Jesus himself, the Son of God, walked on water, calmed storms, and raised the dead, all through the power of his unwavering faith in his Father's will. He taught his disciples that faith, even as small as a mustard seed, could move mountains, demonstrating that faith, regardless of its size, possesses immense power. (Matthew 17:20-21)

    Faith is not merely a passive belief; it is a dynamic force that ignites action, transforms circumstances, and unlocks divine potential. When we exercise our faith, we tap into the infinite power of God, enabling us to overcome seemingly insurmountable obstacles and experience His supernatural intervention in our lives. The power of faith lies not in our own strength or abilities but in our willingness to surrender to God's will and trust in His promises. It is a constant choice to believe, to hope, and to trust, even when our circumstances seem hopeless. Faith requires us to let go of our own understanding and embrace God's plan, trusting that He knows what is best, even when we cannot see it.

    Faith is not a shield that protects us from trials and

Chapter 08

tribulations; rather, it is the armor that empowers us to face them head-on, knowing that we are not alone. It is the confidence that comes from knowing that God is with us, fighting for us, and guiding our steps. The journey of faith is not without its challenges. Doubt and fear may tempt us to question God's presence and His promises. But in these moments of doubt, we test and refine our faith. We must cling to the promises of God, remembering His faithfulness throughout history and His steadfast love for us.

 We must remember that faith is a gift from God, not something we earn or achieve on our own. The Holy Spirit bestows upon us a supernatural power that enables us to trust in God's goodness, love, and faithfulness. We can ask God for faith, and He will generously provide it, just as He provides all other spiritual gifts.

 The power of faith is evident in the lives of countless believers who have experienced miraculous breakthroughs and overcome seemingly insurmountable challenges. These testimonies remind us that faith is more than a belief. It is a

Chapter 08

force that can transform our lives. Through faith, we can walk on water, calm storms, and overcome any obstacle that comes our way. Faith is the key to unlocking God's power in our lives, enabling us to experience His love, peace, and guidance, even in the darkest of times.

In the words of the Apostle Paul, "For I am convinced that neither death nor life, neither angels nor demons, neither the present nor the future, nor any powers, neither height nor depth, nor anything else in all creation, will be able to separate us from the love of God that is in Christ Jesus our Lord." (Romans 8:38-39)

Let us embrace the power of faith, knowing that it is our most powerful weapon in spiritual warfare. Let us stand firm in our belief, knowing that God is with us, fighting for us, and leading us towards victory. Let us allow faith to be our anchor, guiding us through the storms of life and leading us to the shores of eternal hope.

Chapter 09
Overcoming Fear and Doubt

Fear and doubt, like unwelcome shadows, can creep into our hearts, casting a chill over our faith and hindering our progress in the spiritual realm. It's tempting to let these insidious emotions paralyze us, preventing us from stepping forward and claiming the victories that God has promised. Yet, Scripture reminds us that we are not to be overcome by fear, but to walk in the power and authority that Christ has bestowed upon us. As a seasoned warrior faces battles with unwavering courage,

Chapter 09

so too must we confront the fears and doubts that seek to hold us captive. Our weapon in this spiritual warfare is not physical strength or worldly wisdom, but the unwavering faith in God's power, His love, and His promises. Let us embrace the truth that He is our shield, our refuge, and our source of strength.

Remember the story of Gideon, a seemingly insignificant man whom God called to deliver Israel from the Midianites. Overwhelmed by the magnitude of the task, Gideon questioned God's ability to use him. Yet, God reassured him, saying, "Go in the strength that I have given you." Gideon, fueled by faith, was ultimately victorious.

Similarly, our fears and doubts are often rooted in a lack of trust in God's ability to work in our lives. We may feel tempted to rely on our own strength and understanding, but we forget that in our weakness, God's power is made perfect. It is essential to acknowledge our limitations and surrender to the divine power that resides within us through the Holy Spirit.

Chapter 09

The Bible is replete with stories of individuals who faced seemingly insurmountable challenges, yet through faith and obedience, they overcame fear and achieved remarkable victories. Consider the apostle Paul, who endured imprisonment, persecution, and numerous trials throughout his ministry. Despite these hardships, his unwavering faith remained steadfast, enabling him to proclaim the gospel with unyielding courage. When fear and doubt cloud our minds, it's crucial to seek refuge in prayer and the Word of God.

Prayer is our lifeline to the throne of grace, a conduit through which we can pour out our anxieties and receive God's comforting presence and guidance. We must diligently study the Scriptures, allowing the words of truth and promise to ignite our faith and dispel the darkness of fear. The Scriptures offer countless verses that promise strength and protection in times of fear. Here are a few that can serve as powerful reminders:

Chapter 09

"Be strong and courageous. Do not be afraid; do not be discouraged, for the Lord your God will be with you wherever you go." (Joshua 1:9)

"The Lord is my shepherd; I shall not want. He makes me lie downin green pastures; He leads me beside quiet waters; He refreshes my soul." (Psalm 23:1-3)

"Do not be anxious about anything, but in every situation, by prayer and petition, with thanksgiving, present your requests to God. And the peace of God, which transcends all understanding, will guard your hearts and your minds in Christ Jesus." (Philippians 4:6-7)

Remember, faith is not the absence of fear, but a choice to trust God even in the face of it. Fear is a natural human emotion, but it should not be allowed to dictate our actions or cloud our perspective. Embrace the power of God's promises, allowing them to infuse your heart with courage and confidence. We are not alone in this spiritual battle. We have a mighty warrior in Christ who has already overcome the world. His victory is our

Chapter 09

victory, and His strength is our strength. Let us lean on His power and trust in His promises, knowing that with Him, we can face any challenge with boldness and faith.

Cultivating a steadfast heart requires a conscious effort to build our faith muscles. Just as consistent exercise builds physical strength, consistent prayer, meditation on God's Word, and reliance on His power foster spiritual resilience.

Here are some practical steps to overcome fear and cultivate confidence in God's power:

1. Acknowledge Your Fear: Don't suppress or deny your fears. Instead, bring them to the Lord in prayer. Confess your fears to Him, and ask for His guidance and strength to overcome them.

2. Focus on God's Promises: Spend time meditating on verses that speak to your specific fears. Allow these promises to become a stronghold in your heart, anchoring you in times of uncertainty.

3. Practice Gratitude: Cultivating a grateful heart can help shift our focus away from fear and onto God's goodness. Make a

Chapter 09

habit of expressing gratitude for the blessings in your life, big and small.

4. Engage in Spiritual Warfare: Remember that fear often originates from spiritual attacks. Engage in spiritual warfare through prayer, fasting, and the use of the Armor of God.

5. Surround Yourself with Faith-Filled People: Connect with other believers who can encourage you, pray with you, and support your spiritual journey.

6. Celebrate Your Victories: Take time to acknowledge and celebrate even small victories. God's faithfulness is often revealed in the smallest of triumphs.

7. Choose to Trust: Trust in God's sovereign plan, even when you don't understand it. Remember that He is working all things together for your good.

8. Remember God's Love: Never forget that God loves you unconditionally. His love for you is a source of strength and comfort in the midst of fear and uncertainty.

In the face of fear, it's easy to feel helpless and alone.

Chapter 09

However, we must remember that we are not fighting this battle alone. We have a loving and powerful God who is always with us, ready to empower us, protect us, and guide us. Remember, faith is not a feeling but a decision. It's a choice to trust God even when you don't feel like it. It's a choice to believe in His promises even when your circumstances suggest otherwise.

    Let's choose to walk in the strength that God has given us, knowing that He will never leave us nor forsake us. We are more than conquerors through Him who loved us. May these words encourage you to overcome fear and step into the fullness of God's power in your life. Remember, "The Lord is my light and my salvation—whom shall I fear? The Lord is the stronghold of my life—of whom shall I be afraid?" (Psalm 27:1)

Chapter 10
Stories of Light in Darkness

In the tapestry of life, where shadows dance and light struggles to penetrate, there exist moments when the darkness seems to consume everything. These times test the very foundations of our faith, and the whispers of doubt attempt to drown out the comforting voice of hope. It is in these depths of despair that the hand of God reaches out, offering a lifeline of grace and intervention.

Imagine a young woman named Sarah, a devoted

Chapter 10

Christian, enduring a harrowing ordeal. The doctors had diagnosed her with a terminal illness, leaving her shattered and filled with fear. The doctors had given her only a few months to live, and the weight of her impending fate pressed heavily upon her. Sarah's faith, once a beacon of strength, was now flickering in the face of such immense pain and uncertainty. She cried out to God, pleading for a miracle, her voice trembling with both desperation and hope.

    As days turned into weeks, Sarah found herself in a desperate search for solace. She spent hours in prayer, her heart overflowing with sorrow and yearning for divine intervention. It was during one such prayer session that she felt a profound shift within her. A sense of calmness washed over her, and a voice, soft yet distinct, spoke to her soul. "My child, do not fear. I am with you. I will heal you." This was not a hallucination but a tangible experience, a revelation of God's presence in her darkest hour. The voice filled her with an inexplicable peace and renewed hope. She felt a surge of faith welling up within her,

Chapter 10

replacing the fear that had been her constant companion. From that moment, Sarah's outlook on life transformed. Her illness remained, but the fear that had gripped her vanished. She found strength in the assurance of God's love and the unwavering promise of healing.

Another such story unfolds in the life of a man named David. He was a successful businessman, yet he found himself wrestling with a deep-seated addiction that threatened to destroy his life. He had tried countless times to break free from its grip, but the power of the addiction always seemed to overpower him. David's life was a chaotic mess, and he felt consumed by shame and despair. One fateful day, David stumbled upon a small prayer group. He had been reluctant to seek help, fearing judgment and rejection. But something drew him to that group, a faint hope that maybe, just maybe, he could find a way out of his dark abyss. As he listened to others share their struggles and victories, he realized he was not alone. His heart ached with a longing for freedom, and he began to pray for

Chapter 10

God's deliverance.

It wasn't a sudden transformation, but a slow and gradual process. With each prayer, each step of faith, David felt the chains of addiction loosening their hold on him. He still had his battles, but now he had a community of believers who supported him, prayed with him, and walked beside him through the difficult journey of recovery. The love and encouragement they offered, fueled by their faith, helped him find the strength he needed to overcome the addiction.

These show, in part, the many stories of those who felt God's intervention in their darkest moments. A young woman facing death and a man with an addiction transformed their lives through God's unwavering presence. It revealed His deep love and commitment to His children. These encounters serve as powerful testimonies to the transformative power of faith and prayer. When the world seems to be crumbling around us, when darkness seems to consume all hope, it is in those moments that we must cling to the promise of God's

Chapter 10

intervention. He is not indifferent to our struggles; He is our refuge, our strength, and our unwavering source of hope.

As we journey through life, we may face trials and tribulations that test our faith and challenge our resilience. But remember, we are not alone. God is with us, always. He is the Light in the darkness, the hope in despair, and the source of healing and deliverance. In the words of the apostle Paul, "Therefore, my beloved brethren, be steadfast, immovable, always abounding in the work of the Lord, knowing that your labor is not in vain in the Lord." (1 Corinthians 15:58) Let us embrace the power of prayer, the strength of faith, and the unwavering love of God. Let us stand strong in the face of adversity, knowing that even in the darkest of nights, God is our light and our salvation.

Chapter 11
Deliverance From Setback and Stagnation

Have you ever felt like you were stuck in a rut, like your dreams were fading into the background, replaced by a constant sense of frustration and disappointment? It's like you're carrying a heavy weight, holding you back from reaching your full potential. You pray, you strive, you put in the effort, but it seems like no matter what you do, you're constantly facing setbacks and delays. You may even find yourself caught in a cycle of stagnation, feeling like you're going nowhere.

Chapter 11

This, dear friend, is the very essence of being bound by chains – unseen forces that restrict our progress and steal our joy. The enemy, who seeks to steal, kill, and destroy, delights in hindering our journey, causing us to stumble and lose hope. But the good news is that we can break these chains. God's power and the unshakeable faith that resides within you can shatter and rip them apart.

Breaking free from these chains is not a passive process; it requires an intentional, proactive approach. It's time to engage in spiritual warfare, to raise our voices in prayer and declare our freedom from the shackles that hold us captive. It's time to claim the promises of God, to stand firm in our faith, and to declare our victory over every obstacle that comes our way. Let's begin our journey of liberation by understanding that setbacks and stagnation are not our destiny. They are temporary roadblocks placed in our path by the enemy to discourage us and divert us from our God-given purpose. But we are warriors, equipped with the armor of God, and we have the power to overcome these

Chapter 11

hindrances through prayer and unwavering faith.

The Importance of Prayer

Prayer is the cornerstone of our spiritual warfare, the very weapon we use to break free from the chains that bind us. It is a powerful force that can move mountains, change circumstances, and release the chains that have held us captive for so long. When we pray, we are entering into communion with God, aligning ourselves with His will and accessing His infinite power. We are tapping into a source of strength that surpasses human understanding, a force that can overcome any obstacle and shatter any chains.

Effective Prayers for Deliverance

The Bible is replete with examples of people who overcame seemingly insurmountable challenges through prayer. They persevered through hardship, holding fast to their faith, and received divine intervention. We can do the same!

Here are some powerful prayers that can help you break free from setbacks and stagnation:

Chapter 11

1. The Prayer of Repentance:

"Oh Lord, I come before you today, acknowledging my sin and seeking your forgiveness. I repent of any actions that have hindered your blessings in my life. I ask for your cleansing and your restoration, and I commit to living a life that pleases you."

2. The Prayer of Declaration:

"Lord, I declare that I am free from the chains of setbacks and stagnation. I break the power of every demonic influence that seeks to hinder my progress. I claim Your promises of abundance, joy, and fulfillment in every area of my life."

3. The Prayer of Protection:

"Lord, I ask for your protection from any further attacks. I place my life under your covering, and I trust in your faithfulness to shield me from harm."

4. The Prayer of Perseverance:

"Lord, give me strength to persevere through any challenges that come my way. Grant me wisdom to discern Your will and courage to stand firm in my faith, even in the face of adversity."

Chapter 11

5. The Prayer of Thanksgiving:

"Lord, thank You for Your faithfulness and Your love."

Thank you for your constant presence and your unwavering support. I am grateful for your promises of victory, and I trust in your perfect plan for my life.

Practices for Breaking Free

Prayer is not a magic formula; it is a powerful tool that requires us to actively engage in spiritual warfare. Here are some additional practices that can help us break free from setbacks and stagnation:

1. Repentance:

We must examine our hearts and lives, confessing any sin that may be hindering our progress. God's forgiveness is essential for removing the chains of guilt and shame that can hold us back.

2. Fasting and Prayer:

Fasting is a spiritual discipline that can amplify our prayers and draw us closer to God. It allows us to focus our hearts and minds on seeking His will and breaking the chains that bind us.

Chapter 11

3. Bible Study and Meditation:

Immersing ourselves in God's Word and meditating on His promises empowers us with the strength and wisdom to overcome challenges.

4. Praise and Worship:

Praising God and lifting our voices in worship is a powerful weapon against the enemy. It creates an atmosphere of joy and victory that dispels darkness and breaks the chains of despair.

5. Walking in Obedience:

When we obey God's word and align our lives with His will, we are living in freedom. Obedience breaks the chains of sin and allows us to walk in the fullness of His blessings.

Breaking the Cycle of Stagnation

The cycle of stagnation is a vicious trap that can leave us feeling defeated and hopeless. However, God's grace is sufficient to break this cycle and restore us to our rightful place of joy and fulfillment.

Chapter 11

Here are some key steps to breaking the cycle of stagnation:

1. Identify the root causes:

We must first identify the root causes of our stagnation. What are the areas in our lives that feel stuck? What are the patterns that keep us from moving forward? Once we identify these areas, we can begin to pray specifically for deliverance.

2. Seek God's Direction:

Ask God to reveal His plan for your life, to show you the path He desires you to walk. Be willing to surrender your will to His, and trust in His perfect timing.

3. Embrace Change:

Stagnation often arises from resistance to change. Be willing to let go of the old and embrace the new. Trust that God is working for your good, even when things seem uncertain.

4. Cultivate a Growth Mindset:

Develop a growth mindset, believing that you have the capacity to learn, grow, and evolve. Don't be afraid to step out of your comfort zone and take risks.

Chapter 11

5. Stay Connected to God:

Maintain a consistent relationship with God through prayer, Bible study, and fellowship with other believers. This connection will provide you with the strength and support you need to overcome any obstacles.

Stories of Freedom

     Throughout history and in our own lives, we find countless stories of individuals who have overcome the chains of setbacks and stagnation. These stories are a testament to God's power, His love, and His desire to set us free. Remember the Israelites in Egypt, burdened by slavery and oppression. Through Moses' courageous faith and God's divine intervention, they were miraculously delivered from bondage, experiencing a transformation that set them on a journey to the Promised Land. Consider David, a young shepherd who faced a formidable giant, Goliath, with nothing but a slingshot and faith in God. He stood firm in the face of adversity, trusting in God's power and emerging victorious.

Chapter 11

These stories, along with countless others, remind us that we are not alone in our struggles. God is with us every step of the way, ready to break every chain and set us free. We are not defined by our setbacks or our struggles. Our faith in God, His love for us, and His desire to see us thrive define us.

A Life of Abundance

When we break free from the chains that bind us, we step into a life of abundance – an overflowing life of joy, purpose, and fulfillment. We are no longer held back by the enemy's schemes. We empower ourselves to pursue our God-given dreams, to live with boldness and purpose, and to experience the fullness of God's blessings. This journey of freedom is not without its challenges, but with God by our side, we can overcome any obstacle. We can shatter the chains of setbacks and stagnation and embrace the life of abundance that God has prepared for us.

In the words of Isaiah 61:1-4, "The Spirit of the Sovereign Lord is on me, because the Lord has anointed me to proclaim

Chapter 11

good news to the poor. He has sent me to bind up the brokenhearted, to proclaim freedom for the captives and release from darkness for the prisoners. To proclaim the year of the Lord's favor and the day of vengeance of our God, to comfort all who mourn, and provide for those who grieve in Zion—to bestow on them a crown of beauty instead of ashes, the oil of joy instead of mourning, and a garment of praise instead of a spirit of despair." Let us embrace these words with faith, and let us walk boldly into the freedom that God has prepared for us. Let us break free from the chains of setbacks and stagnation, and experience the transformative power of His love and grace.

Chapter 12
Prayers For Overcoming Delays

The enemy, in his cunning and deceitfulness, often employs tactics that delay our progress and hinder our spiritual advancement. He wants to discourage us, make us doubt God's promises, and keep us stuck in a cycle of frustration and despair. But remember, God is our ultimate guide, our protector, and our provider. He desires our flourishing, our growth, and our ultimate victory. Therefore, we must rise above the tactics of the enemy and engage in fervent prayer, pleading for God's

Chapter 12

intervention to break the chains of delay and usher us into a season of divine acceleration. Let's begin by acknowledging our dependence on God, confessing our need for His divine intervention, and asking for His wisdom to understand the root causes of these delays.

Prayer for Open Doors and Divine Favor:

"Heavenly Father, I come before You today, recognizing Your power and authority over every circumstance. I acknowledge that You are the God who opens doors and no man can shut them. I ask that You break every barrier that stands in my way, every hindrance that is delaying my progress. Open the doors of opportunity, favor, and blessing. Let Your presence pave the way for me, and grant me Your divine favor in every aspect of my life. In Jesus' mighty name, I pray."

Prayer for Spiritual Alignment:

"Lord, I recognize that sometimes my delays are a consequence of misalignment with Your will. I seek Your guidance, Your direction, and Your wisdom. Help me to discern Your plan for

Chapter 12

my life and to embrace it fully, aligning my actions with Your divine purpose. Break every pattern of disobedience, every stubbornness, and every resistance in my heart. Let me be a willing vessel, fully surrendered to Your will and Your timing. I ask for Your grace, Your strength, and Your supernatural power to overcome any obstacle that stands in the way of Your perfect plan for my life. Amen."

Prayer Against Demonic Influence:

"Father, I declare that I am a child of light, and I reject the darkness that seeks to control me and hinder my progress. I renounce any demonic influence affecting me, any curses placed upon me, and any evil spirits manipulating my circumstances. I claim the authority given to me in Your name, Jesus, and I command every delaying spirit to be bound and cast out of my life. I decree that Your presence fills my life, replacing darkness with light and ushering in Your divine favor in Jesus' mighty name, I pray."

Prayer for Supernatural Speed:

"Oh God, You are the God of miracles, the God who can do

Chapter 12

exceedingly, abundantly above all that we ask or think. I believe that You have a destiny for my life, a plan of success and prosperity. I ask for Your supernatural acceleration, Your divine speed in all areas of my life. I pray that You break every delay, every roadblock, and every obstacle. Let Your favor open doors and Your power propel me forward with unprecedented speed. I am not content with mediocrity; I desire to walk in Your fullness and experience the abundant life You have promised. Amen."

Engage in the Word and Be Filled with God's Promises:

Beyond fervent prayers, immersing yourself in God's Word and meditating on His promises is essential. The Bible is a source of wisdom, hope, and spiritual power. "For the word of God is living and active. Sharper than any double-edged sword, it penetrates even to dividing soul and spirit, joints and marrow; it judges the thoughts and attitudes of the heart." (Hebrews 4:12) "Now to him who is able to do immeasurably more than all we ask or imagine, according to his power that is at work

Chapter 12

within us..." (Ephesians 3:20) As you spend time in prayer, seeking God's guidance, remember these verses and allow them to nourish your spirit, strengthen your faith, and guide you toward victory.

Let us Declare God's Truth:

Delays are not the end. They are an opportunity to seek God's face, to align our hearts with His will, and to experience His transformative power. "The Lord is not slow in keeping His promise, as some understand slowness. Instead, he is patient with you, not wanting anyone to perish, but wanting everyone to come to repentance." (2 Peter 3:9)

    Remember that God is sovereign, and His timing is always perfect. Trust His promises, believe in His faithfulness, and know that He will bring His plans to fruition in His perfect time. As you engage in these prayers, hold fast to the promises of God, and watch as He breaks the chains of delay, ushering you into a season of divine breakthroughs.

Chapter 13
Healing from Past Wounds

The scars of our past can linger, casting long shadows over our present and hindering our future. As physical wounds need time and care to heal, so too do the emotional and spiritual wounds that we carry. These wounds can manifest in various forms: betrayal, abuse, loss, trauma, or simply the weight of our own mistakes. They can leave us feeling broken, unworthy, and disconnected from God's love and grace. However, we will not let these wounds define us.

Chapter 13

Through the transformative power of prayer, we can embark on a journey of healing and restoration. The Bible reminds us in Psalm 147:3, "He heals the brokenhearted and binds up their wounds." God is a compassionate healer who desires to mend our brokenness and bring us wholeness. This journey of healing starts with acknowledging our wounds. We cannot ignore them, bury them, or pretend they don't exist. Acknowledging our pain is the first step toward facing it and allowing God to work in our hearts. It can be a difficult process, but it is essential for releasing the grip these wounds have on our lives.

Next, we need to open our hearts to God's love and forgiveness. He is a God of second chances, and He offers us His grace unconditionally. Forgiveness, of ourselves and others, is key to breaking the chains of bitterness, anger, and resentment that often follow past wounds. Prayer becomes our lifeline in this process. It's not a magical solution, but a profound act of communion with God, where we pour out our hearts, our pain,

Chapter 13

our struggles, and our longing for healing. Through prayer, we surrender our wounds to God, trusting His power to heal and restore us.

Here are some key areas of prayer that can guide our journey to healing:

Praying for Emotional Healing:

Acknowledging the Pain: Start by simply acknowledging the pain you are carrying. Don't try to minimize it or pretend it's not there. Be honest with God about your feelings.

Seek Forgiveness: If betrayal or abuse has caused the wounds, pray for the strength to forgive both yourself and the other person. Remember, forgiveness is not about condoning the wrong but about releasing yourself from the bitterness that binds you.

Embracing Acceptance: Pray for acceptance of your past and the events that have shaped you. Recognize that the past is a part of your story, but it doesn't have to define you. Asking for Strength: Pray for the strength to move forward and overcome

Chapter 13

the lingering effects of these wounds. Ask God to give you the courage to face your fears and to build resilience.

Praying for Spiritual Healing:

- **Seeking Restoration of Your Relationship with God:** If your wounds have created a sense of distance from God, pray for the restoration of your relationship with Him. Ask Him to help you rediscover your faith and rekindle your love for Him.

- **Repentance:** Pray for forgiveness for any past mistakes or actions that contributed to your pain. Remember that God's grace is always available to those who seek it.

- **Seeking God's Guidance:** Pray for God's guidance as you navigate the healing process. Ask for wisdom, understanding, and discernment as you make decisions about your future.

Praying for Strength and Hope:

- **Praying for a Renewed Mind:** Pray for a renewed mind, free from negative thoughts, self-defeating patterns, and the influence of the enemy.

Chapter 13

- **Praying for Peace:** Pray for inner peace and serenity. Let God's love wash over you and soothe your troubled heart.
- **Praying for Joy and Hope:** Pray for joy and hope to fill your heart, even in the midst of pain and struggle. Remind yourself of God's promises for your life, and embrace the hope of a future filled with healing and wholeness.

Healing from past wounds is a journey, not a destination. It takes time, patience, and faith. There will be moments of setbacks and struggles, but with God's help, you can overcome them.

Here are some practical steps to supplement your prayer journey:

- **Seek Professional Help:** If you are struggling with deep emotional wounds, consider seeking help from a therapist, counselor, or spiritual mentor. They can provide valuable support and guidance as you work through your pain.

Chapter 13

- **Join a Support Group:** Connecting with others who have experienced similar wounds can offer a sense of community, understanding, and encouragement.
- **Engage in Self-Care:** Make time for activities that nourish your body, mind, and spirit. This could include exercise, healthy eating, spending time in nature, reading uplifting books, or listening to inspiring music.
- **Practice Gratitude:** Take time to acknowledge the good things in your life, even during difficult times. Gratitude can shift your focus from pain to hope.
- **Serve Others:** Helping others can be a powerful way to break free from self-absorption and find meaning in your journey.

Remember, you are not alone. God is with you every step of the way. He sees your pain, understands your struggles, and commits to your healing. Through prayer, faith, and the guidance of the Holy Spirit, you can break free from the chains of your past and walk toward a brighter future.

Glossary

This glossary provides definitions of key terms and concepts used throughout the book:

Altars: Spiritual constructs or places where demonic entities can operate and exert influence.

Deliverance: The act of being set free from demonic oppression, bondage, or spiritual attacks.

Demons: Evil spirits that are antagonistic to God and seek to harm or deceive humans.

Spiritual Warfare: The conflict between the forces of light (God and His followers) and the forces of darkness (demons and evil spirits).

Strongholds: Spiritual fortifications built by demonic forces in a person's life, hindering their progress and well-being.

Witchcraft: The use of supernatural power for evil purposes, including casting spells and curses.

Sylvia Blessings loves sharing her journey, inspirations, and encouragement with her readers. Join her vibrant online community and be the first to hear about new projects, events, and more!

Follow Sylvia on Social Media

- Instagram: @sylvia_blessings
- Facebook: Rev. Sylvia Blessings
- YouTube: Sylvia Blessings TV

Quick Connect

Let's inspire and grow together—one story at a time.

www.ingramcontent.com/pod-product-compliance
Lightning Source LLC
Chambersburg PA
CBHW072202160426
43197CB00012B/2494